BIG-NOTE PIANO

the twilight saga

eclipse

THE SCORE
MUSIC BY HOWARD SHORE

ISBN 978-1-4234-9652-6

HAL•LEONARD®
CORPORATION

7777 W. BLUEMOUND RD. P.O. BOX 13819 MILWAUKEE, WI 53213

In Australia Contact:
Hal Leonard Australia Pty. Ltd.
4 Lentara Court
Cheltenham, Victoria, 3192 Australia
Email: ausadmin@halleonard.com.au

Visit Hal Leonard Online at
www.halleonard.com

COMPROMISE/BELLA'S THEME

Music Composed by HOWARD SHORE,
EMILY HAINES and JAMES SHAW

VICTORIA

Composed by
HOWARD SHORE

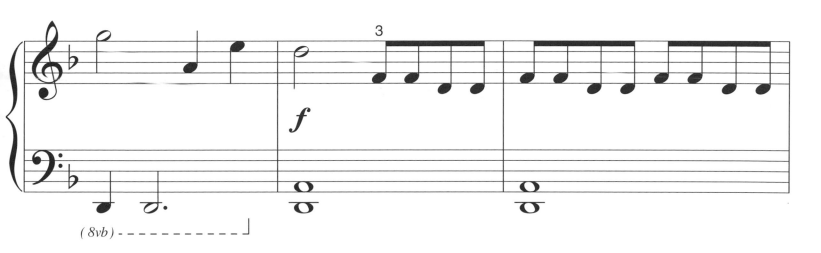

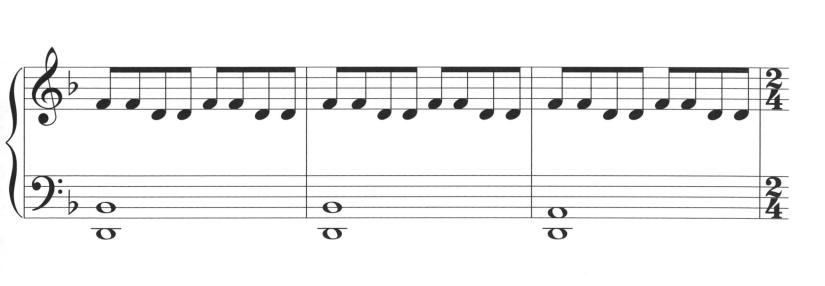

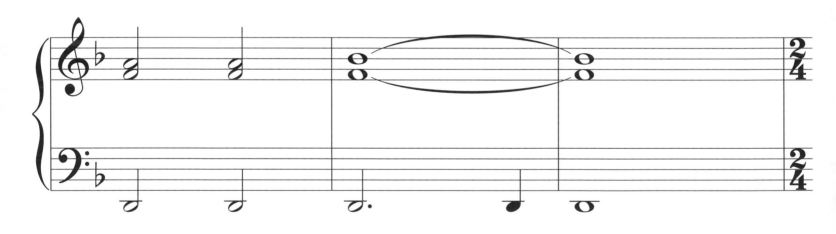

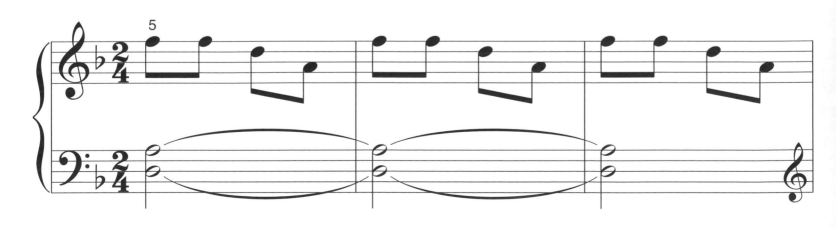

IMPRINTING

Composed by
HOWARD SHORE

Very slowly

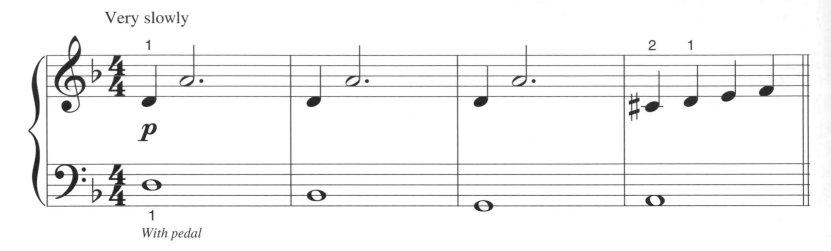

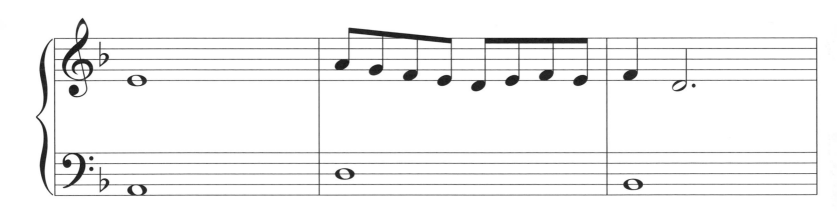

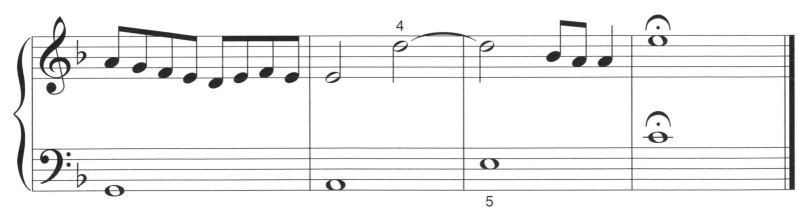

FIRST KISS

Composed by
HOWARD SHORE

Slowly

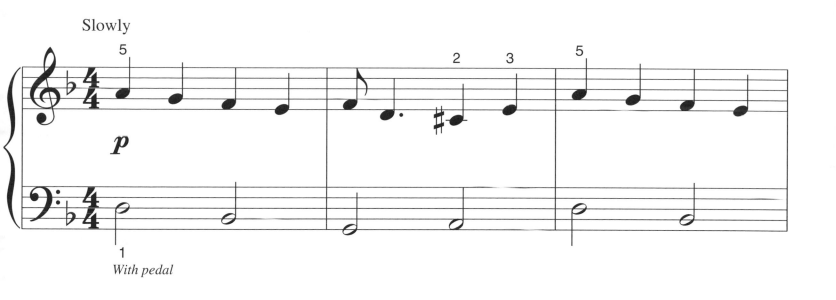

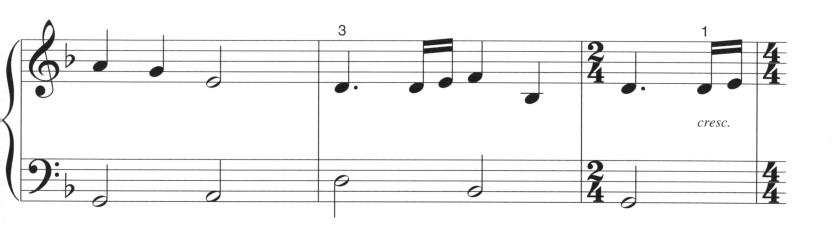

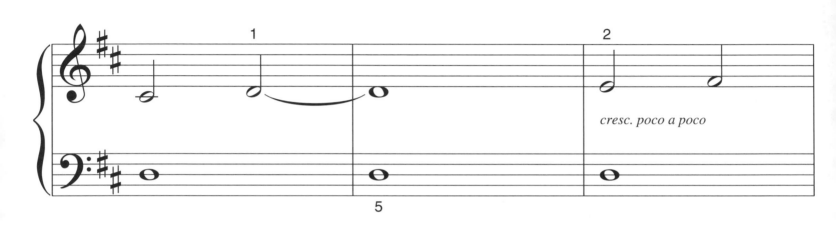

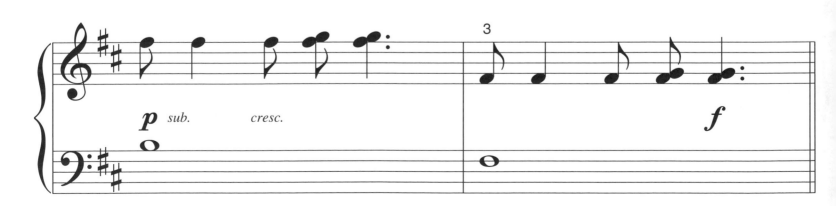

JACOB'S THEME

Composed by
HOWARD SHORE

JASPER

Composed by
HOWARD SHORE

THE KISS

Composed by
HOWARD SHORE

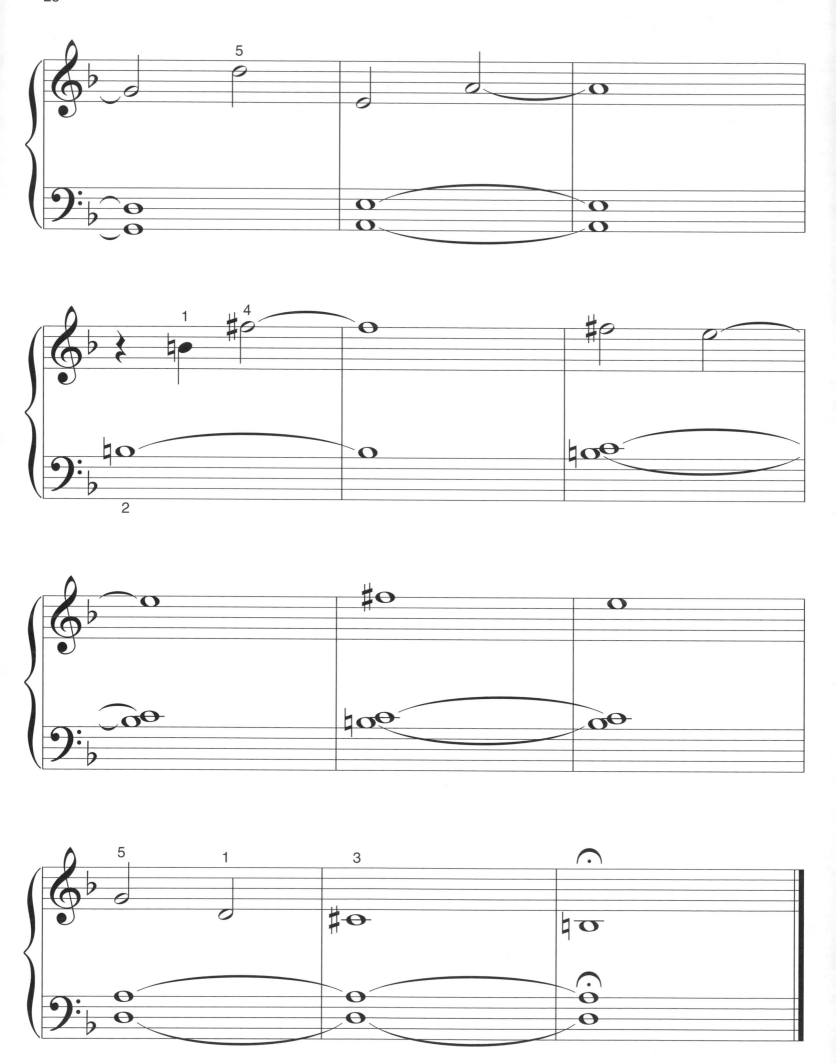

As Easy As Breathing

Composed by
HOWARD SHORE

Slowly, expressively

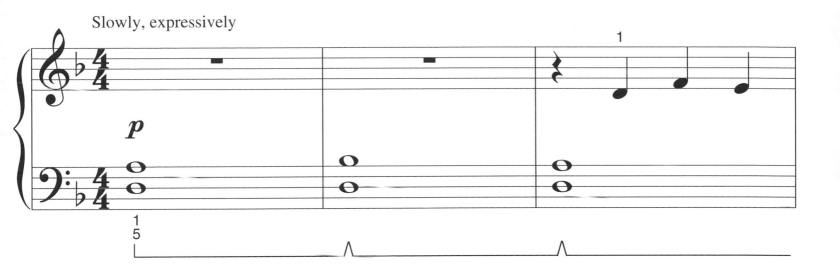

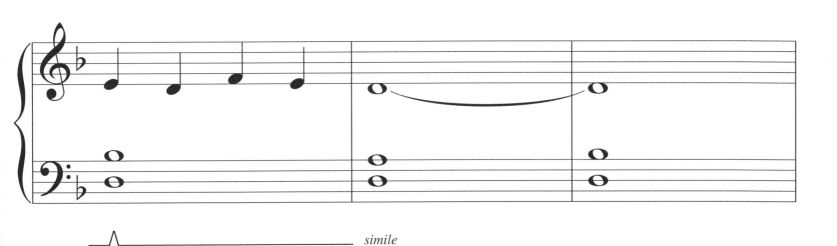

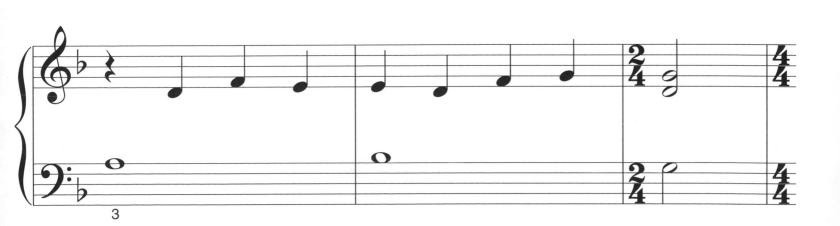

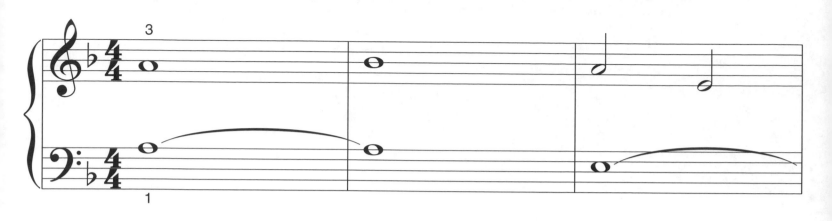

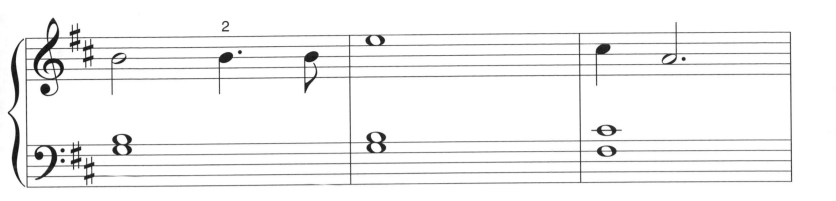

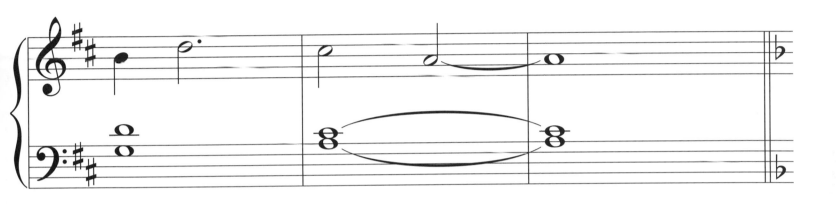

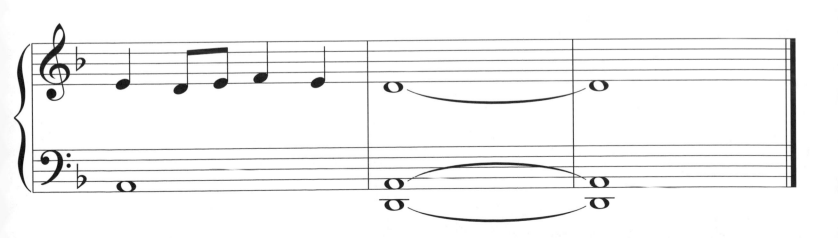

WEDDING PLANS

Music Composed by HOWARD SHORE,
EMILY HAINES and JAMES SHAW

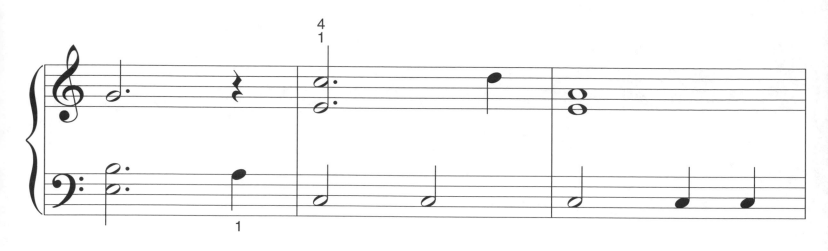

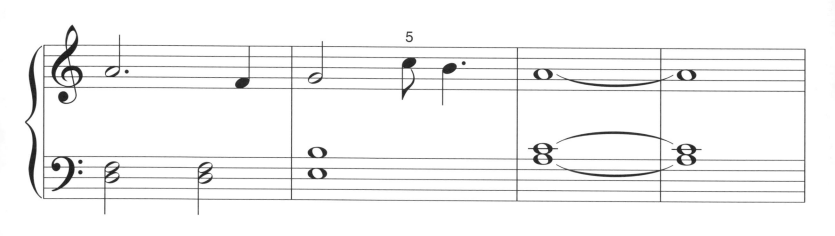

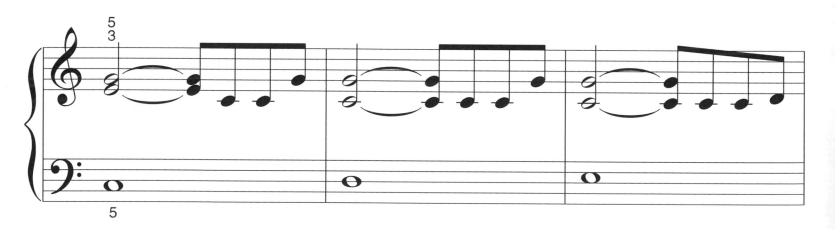

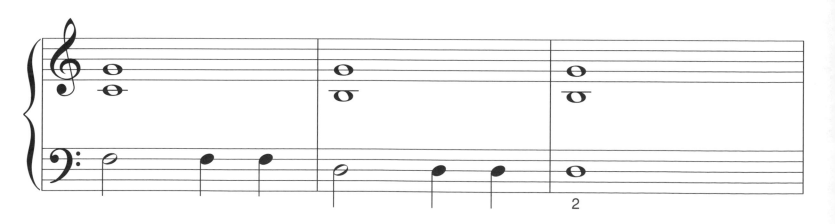

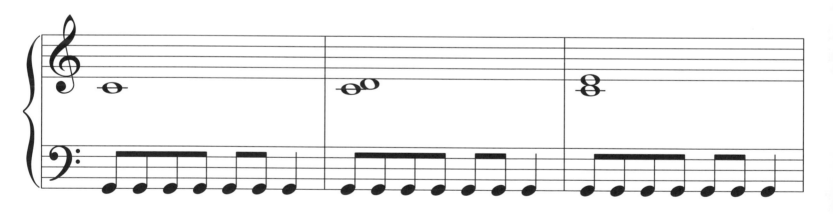

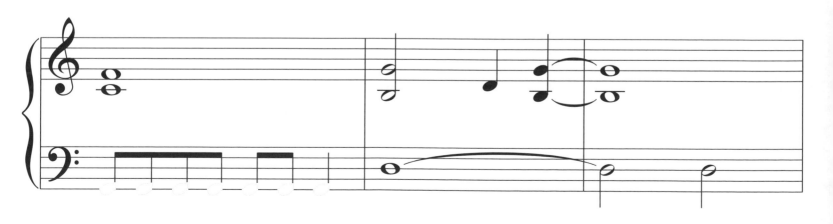

Segue to "Eclipse (All Yours)"

ECLIPSE (ALL YOURS)

Written by EMILY HAINES,
JAMES SHAW and HOWARD SHORE